Invisible Weapons

by Jenks and Brown

DESERT PUBLICATIONS

INVISIBLE WEAPONS

by

Harold J. Jenks
Michael H. Brown

Ⓒ 1979
Desert Publications

ISBN: 0 - 87947 - 429 - 7

DESERT PUBLICATIONS
Cornville, Arizona 86325

TABLE OF CONTENTS

Contents	Page

Theory of Improvised Weapons

In the middle and late twentieth century there is and has been a considerable interest in improvised weapons in the ranks of the martial arts practitioners and para-military buffs. With some people it amounts to little more than a hobby and with others it is a way of anticipating the moves of the present government in its persistent determination to disarm us.

Very few of the men involved actually understand what an improvised weapon is. Fortunately, most of the men who do keep weapons to protect their home and families understand what a professional weapon is. However, very few improvised weapons are a match for a rifle, shotgun, or pistol, although there is some overlap.

For example, a Colt revolver is a professional weapon when it contains a cylinder full of live rounds and the man with his hand on the butt and finger on the trigger is either firing it or using it to control a situation. If the same man with the same gun is in a bar-room brawl or similar hand to hand encounter, afraid to pull the trigger for fear of hitting his friends, and using the weapon as a club instead; it is then an improvised weapon.

On the other hand there are certain items, especially among the martial arts crowd, that were originally tools or other devices that reached such a high degree of sophistication used as a weapon that they can now be considered professional weapons. For example, the nun-chaku was once used in Okinawa to pound and make flour. In most areas of the United States it is now considered a club, a deadly weapon, and some of the criminal penalties for just carrying it, let alone using it, make carrying a machinegun with a belt of live ammunition a lot more practical. One unfortunate in Texas wound up with five years in prison in 1977 just for driving around with one on the front seat of his car.

An improvised or invisible weapon should be one that normally wouldn't be considered a weapon at any time. It should be fairly obvious that a baseball bat wouldn't apply. It is a very effective weapon and will do well in a pinch but there is a major drawback to using one. If you're driving to or from baseball practice you might be covered legally but if you lay out a dozen people at a Drive-In Movie with it you may have some difficult explaining to do to a judge and a jury.

The things to look for are items you run across constantly in the normal course of a day's events. Ashtrays, ballpoint pens, telephones, hot coffee, drinking glasses, and the like. Even a wall, water fountain, or the top of a desk make excellent spur-of-the-moment weapons if you know how to use them. It's all a matter of knowing a few of the basics and then being able to think on your feet when the occasion warrents it.

The Weapons of Okinawa

A lot of would-be self-defense fans in the United States spend a lot of time, effort, and money in learning the self-defense methods of ancient Okinawa. Unfortunately, most of the weapons used in ancient Okinawa are not as easily disguised now as they were then. Use almost anyone of them now in any type of altercation and you have two criminal charges to contend with instead of one (or none): assault with a deadly weapon and carrying a concealed deadly weapon. In some states, like Texas, you might be better off carrying a pistol.

For those not familiar with the methods and weapons that came out of occupied Okinawa, a few are listed and described:

Karate. Despite all the mystique and propaganda surrounding this method the word translates from the Oriental into English as "boxing." In Thailand one version is translated "kick boxing." Which is about what it amounts to.

Bo. This consists of a long staff, tapered at each end. In one recent Hollywood epic the hero wades in a bar with one of these things and proceeds to "clean house." Naturally, the hero emerges victorious and nobody so much as throws an ashtray at him.

The Okinawans used the long staff to carry buckets of water to irrigate their fields. That was the primary function. It also served as a staff. Nor was the staff as a fighting weapon unknown to Europeans. Pick up a Robin Hood book some time and you can read about how Robin's men got in fights with them while Richard the Lion-Hearted was away fighting the Crusades in the early 13th century.

You might be able to use a mop or broom handle today to similar effect if you're not too obvious about it. You might look a little strange wandering in and out of the disco scene carrying a broom handle and wearing your John Travolta clothes.

Nun-chuks. Two forearm-length pieces of hardwood bound together by a foot long length of rope or chain. The idea is to hold one of the pieces of wood, use the "crack-the-whip" effect of the rope or chain, and clobber your opponent with the other free swinging piece. In most United States courts they are classified as clubs and illegal to carry, let alone use.

In ancient Okinawa the nun-chuks were used to pound grain. Presumably the length of cord kept the two sticks from becoming separated and made them easier to carry.

Surushin. A length of rope with weights at both ends. Evidently used in the same fashion as the bolo.

Sai. Pronounced "sigh." A funny-looking sort of short sword, very much resembling a shis-ke-bab iron with exaggerated hand guards. It was originally dragged through the soil by one peasant while another would plant seed in the resulting furrow. As a weapon it was useful for fending off a sword attack by an unfriendly samurai. Supposedly the peasant would have one sai in each hand when approached and a third tucked inside a wide belt. Sai number three was for throwing to confuse the swordsman. Why a clod of dirt or a rock wasn't socially acceptable is anyone's guess.

The sai was also used for killing or maiming someone with a blow to the back of the neck or a thrust to the throat or eye. The ones you see in the karate tournaments these days are not sharpened to a point like the originals.

The principles of improvised weapons seem to remain fairly similar over the centuries. That is, if they work and are not the vain imaginings of some self-appointed self-defense "expert," of which the field seems to have an inordinate number.

For example, on page 53 of our book on knife fighting, BLOODY IRON, the man shows the correct way to hold a knife during an altercation: quillons horizontal and thumb

4

on the blade. It's a method Jenks learned in actual knife fights.

In a book titled, SAI: KARATE WEAPON OF SELF-DEFENSE by Fumio Demura, sold through BLACK BELT magazine, the author shows the proper method for gripping the sai, a grip used for centuries, as identical to the one we advocated in our book. Mr. Demura's instructions are somewhat more comprehensive than ours. See page 17 of this book.

Neither of us had seen this book until after ours was in its second printing.

* * *

How did Okinawa wind up as the improvised weapons capital of the world? Basically, for the same reasons all the patriotic types in the United States fear gun control. There are a lot of parallels.

Up until 14th century the island was a basically feudal society, with lords, men-at-arms, and serfs, very similar to the system existing in Europe at the time.

In the 15th century a man named Sho Shin became king. He was powerful enough in his own right to shove major organizational changes down the throats of everyone concerned. His first step was to pass an edict that swords would no longer be worn as personal equipment. At the time the Japanese system or manner of wearing two swords was prevelant.

The king's next move was to order all the lords to bring all their weapons to the king's castle at Shuri, to be stored in a warehouse under supervision of one of the king's officers. Sounds sort of like gun registration, confiscation, and the rest, doesn't it?

Finally the nobility itself was asked to move into Shuri to take up residence near the castle, leaving subordinates to manage their estates in their place. After a few years the subordinates were replaced by the king's own men. Metro government doesn't appear to be anything new either.

Japan wasn't far behind. In 1586 and 1587 Toyotomi Hideyoshi pulled the same stunt with his now famous (or infamous) "Sword Edicts." In 1634 Tokugawa Iemitsu compelled the feudal lords of Japan to maintain residence at the shogun's capital.

Most of this nonsene was perpetrated to prevent insurrection. How miserably it failed can be attested to by any student of either Japanese or Okinawan history.

The Okinawans paid the price of their stupidity in February, 1609. A Japanese war-lord named Satsuma with one hundred war junks and 3,000 men moved against the island. There were some preliminary skirmishes along the way.

By April 5, 1609 the Japanese were in full control of Shuri castle. The Okinawans had been no match for them. Their citizens were totally untrained and inexperienced since all the weapons had been put away two centuries earlier. Okinawa became a captive nation.

No evidence has ever been unearthed that the Okinawans contemplated an attempt to throw off the Japanese controls. Which didn't stop the Japanese. An elaborate system of informers and spies, known then as metsuke, was set up, Satsuma abolished the Shuri swordsmithy in 1669, which made swords for ceremonial use only, and in 1669 forbade the import of weapons of any kind. Any weapon used from then on had to be an improvised or invisible one.

On June 6, 1853 Commodore Perry of the U.S. Navy and a detachment of Marines simply walked into Shuri Castle uninvited and unwelcome. The Okinawans couldn't do anything about it. They had no weapons. The Commodore requested permission of the U.S. Government to take over the island as a "protectorate." It certainly would have been easy enough. The Government told him to back off: it seems the British, the French, and the Russians had similar ideas and our Navy was simply not going to get involved in a "king of the hill" situation. Perry's ship was the "Mississippi."

During the battle fought over Okinawa in World War II, the Japanese General Staff occupied Shuri Castle. It wasn't as easy a nut to crack when its defenders were armed. It took three days and nights of 14-inch shells from the World War II battleship "Mississippi" to level the ancient fortress. The General Staff all adjourned to a cave and committed suicide.

The Okinawans themselves were caught between the hammer and the anvil. In the battle itself 12,000 Americans died and the number of wounded exceeded 35,000. 90,401 Japanese soldiers died. Only 4,000 were taken prisoner. 62,489 Okinawans caught in the cross-fire died. One of every eight people in the island.

Centuries of practice with improvised weapons were apparently useless in the face of machine guns, mortars, grenades, and aeriel bombardment.

The Pistol as a Club

A handgun is designed primarily as a short-range weapon for use with bullets. You don't necessarily have to have a loaded weapon to be effective.

Centuries ago most pistols were actually designed to be used as clubs. In the days of matchlock, the wheel-lock, and the early flint-lock most gun makers either attached a round iron ball to the butt of the pistol or cast the handle frame in such a fashion that the butt flared out like a club. The idea was that if the powder charge fizzled for one reason or another the customer would not have the proverbial egg on his face. The weapon could be reversed and held by the barrel, weilded like a club.

Most of the earlier pistols were huge affairs weighing several pounds each. By the middle 18th century flintlock pistols were down to one or two pounds a piece and it was more practical to carry several of them than one monstrosity with a dumbell stuck on one end. John Paul Jones is reputed to have carried six single-shot flintlock pistols in his waist sash for naval battles and he was a small man.

With the invention of the revolver the need for using a pistol as a club in military situations virtually disappeared. The only item necessary on the butt of the pistol was a lanyard ring, a small ring used for connecting or running a piece of leather string through and then around the shoulder of the pistol wearer. The idea was to keep the pistol attached to its user if the user got it knocked out of his hand while falling of a horse.

The lanyard ring is often welded to a .45 clip on the modern Colt .45 Government Automatic. Evidently Colt has a lot of confidence in their clip releases.

Big Jim Cofield, bouncer at the Diamond Club in Dayton, Ohio for 11 years, is a firm believer in using a pistol as a club. On one occasion a girl ran into the Diamond Club screaming, "They've killed me! They've killed me!"

The girl had had all her teeth knocked out.

Big Jim ran outside with a .45 in his hand and a real case of the uglies. The girl had been hit with brass knuckles.

When Jim ran outside he confronted three car loads of guys, all milling around and starting to leave. Jim blew out the front tires of the first car and climbed into the car. He jerked the driver's head to one side, stuck the pistol barrel in his mouth, and told the rest of them he would kill everyone in the car in they moved a muscle. Jim then put knots on everyone's head with the butt end of the gun.

There was no resistance to speak of, he terrorized all twelve men, and then shot out the front tires of the other two cars. All three cars were driven off with the tires flopping around the rims just as fast as they would go.

On another occasion Jenks and the manager of a bar got into a full scale ruckus with an entire football team. Jenks used his .38 caliber pistol as a club to settle most of it.

The bar was in Springfield, Ohio and it was about one o'clock in the morning. A whole football team walked in to celebrate one of their recent victories. The fight started over the jukebox.

One record on the jukebox would stick, when it did one of the football players would slam the jukebox against the wall. The first time the football player slammed it against the wall noone said anything. He tried to play the same song again and the record stuck again. The second time the football player slammed the jukebox as hard as he could.

The manager went up to him and asked him really politely not to break the jukebox, told him there were over 200 selections that didn't stick, and put another quarter in for him.

The football player tried to play the sticking song again.

He kicked the jukebox once again. The manager asked him again not to abuse the jukebox and in turn the football player asked him if he, the manager, wanted to fight. The manager said no and asked him again to behave. The football player started arguing with the manager and followed him back up to the bar. Seven of the football player's friends were at the bar and one of them asked the manager if he wanted to fight. The troublemaker went up to the service area of the bar and started shouting at the manager to come out from behind the bar and fight.

The manager had a can of mace he kept underneath the bar and picked it up, trying to keep the football player talking until he could get the can turned around down at his side so the nozzle would be aimed in the right direction.

Jenks was right beside the manager and knew what was going to happen. He had a .38 Smith & Wesson Heavyweight with a 4" barrel in his pocket. Jenks knew that for the football players to get behind the bar they would either have to go around or jump over. Jenks anticipated that they would try to go around, so he went to the other end of the bar and put his back against the wall. There were about twenty football players.

The manager finally got his can of mace in position and sprayed the football player full in the face. The trouble-maker screamed, backed up, and all the rest of the football players jumped up and ran for the back of the bar. None of them had been watching Jenks and had no idea they were headed right into his .38.

Jenks dropped six of them on the spot. He swung the pistol like a billy club on the first six before they knew what was going on, they went down, and the next three tried to back up. Jenks waded into them and the next three went down.

All it took was a second.

In the next instant the trouble-maker went for something in his back pocket and Jenks thought he was going for a gun. When his hand cleared his pocket Jenks pulled the trigger. He was going for a hankerchief to wipe the mace off his face.

Jenks couldn't keep his gun from going off and so jerked his hand sideways. The bullet didn't hit him. When the gun

11

went off everything stopped. Everyone just stood still.

The individual who started the whole thing still had his eyes full of mace. Two other football players had him by the arms and were going to lead him out the door.

The manager didn't like the idea of the character who started the whole thing just getting away with only tears in his eyes so he went after the trouble-maker with a set of brass knuckles and hit him in the forehead.

The trouble-maker's skin was peeled all the way to the bone in the middle of his forehead, all the way past his hair line. A whole flap of skin could be pulled back and his skull observed.

Several of the football players had to be taken to the hospital. The fight ruined the school football team for a year. One of them had to have a steel plate put in his head the size of a barrel of a .38.

Seven months later Jenks was selling carpet for a friend of his and his friend called him in the office to give him a little news. He had just hired a young woman to work on the telephone as a soliciter and in the course of her pre-employment conversation she mentioned she and her husband were working their way through college, mentioning that her husband had gotten into a fight with some gangsters from Dayton. He was expected to be in the hospital another four or five months in addition to the seven months he had already been in.

Noone went to jail over the fight. Had Jenks shot the football players instead of clubbing them the odds of his staying out of legal trouble would have been many times greater.

Not to mention the fact that a man clubbed with a pistol will usually drop a lot quicker than one who has been shot. Saves ammunition, too.

SOAP

DON'T YOU WISH YOU USED DIAL?

One of the more effective and unrecognizable weapons is the old bar-of-soap-in-a-sock trick. Once the soap is separated from the sock the only way you have to worry about getting busted for using it is if someone sees you in the act. Not so with most other weapons. Guns, brass knuckles, clubs, and the like will incriminate you going and coming. If you're observed with a bloody club folks automatically figure you nailed someone with it. With a bloody sock in your hands most people would think you hurt your foot or are in the process of helping someone who just had an accident.

The most important thing to remember in loading a sock is to avoid certain brands of soap, especially Dial.

In 1962 Jenks was in the federal reformatory in Chillicothe, Ohio, and lived in a dormitory. There were approximately 80 people living in the dormitory. One secluded corner contained six beds, one of which Jenks occupied and another occupied by a little short red-headed fellow from New York. The red-head was about 5'5", blue eyes, very well built, very smart, and a young hot-head. For reasons noone knew he had a personal vendetta with another individual in the dormitory who was from Tennessee. The boy from Tennessee was over six feet, weighed around 220 pounds, with big square head, shoulders, and hands, a real hillbilly. The hillbilly was real well-mannered and never said anything to anybody. Little Red had fought him twice, been whipped twice, and wanted to try again. He asked Jenks what

Load sock by placing a bar of soap inside.

he could do to win the next fight.

Jenks told him to take a couple of bars of soap, tie a knot down at the bottom of the sock to hold the soap in place at the bottom of the sock, and swing it from the other end like a billy club.

So Little Red got a sock, put three bars of soap in it, and tied the knot in it. He waited until the boy from Tennessee was walking down the aisle in between the beds. The boy was going to the shower and all he had on was a pair of shorts, a towel draped across his arm with a wash rag, and

Proper grip, with sock wrapped around hand.

his tooth brush and tooth paste in his hand. He wasn't expecting trouble of any sort.

Little Red ran up behind him, leaped up in the air, and hit the boy from Tennessee as hard as he could with the soap in the sock right square in the middle of the head. Blood squirted up three feet in the air. The hillbilly went down partially to his knees.

Red tried to hit him again but the soap was all pulverized. It was no longer bars, it was just powder.

The hillbilly boy recovered, turned around, and picked

A good improvised face-breaker.

Red up by the arms. He walked Red over to an iron pillar in the dormitory, picked him up, and banged his head against it until he knocked Red out, and let him slide to the floor.

The guards took them both to disciplinary isolation, or the "hole."

When Red got out he was so mad at Jenks he couldn't see straight. He thought Jenks had deliberately tricked him.

The mistake Red made was in using three bars of Dial soap to put in his sock. Dial is not a suitable soap for loading a sock since when you hit something with it it just pulverizes and turns into powder. The type of soap used by convicts in the prisons is institution soap, big heavy bars of harsh soap that most women wouldn't use on a bet. Such bars will smash but they don't break into powder. If you do smash them they will break into chunks, like a sack full of rocks.

Outside of prison the logical soap to use would be Ivory. It's the only soap we know of that won't pulverize if you hit somebody.

This same principle can be used with sand, though in most places there isn't any. You might have a hard time explaining to the police in downtown Chicago what you were doing running with a sock full of sand. The excuses with soap are legion: you thought it was going to rain and a paper bag would get wet and break, the store ran out of paper bags, you found them in someone's trash and your pockets weren't big enough, or you're on your way to your girlfriends house to take a shower with her and you're figuring on using a LOT of soap.

The Hand-Pack

You've probably seen all the juvenile delinquent movies where some young hood puts a roll of quarters in his fist and then proceeds to flail away at his victim.

It's a very effective move even outside the movies.

Make a regular fist. Ball it up. Now hit something fairly solid with it. Notice how the hand or fist "gives"? That's because the hand was not designed to be used as a club and there is an air pocket between the palm of the hand and the fingers even in a tightly balled fist. This is the main reason so many men break their hands on other people's heads.

Now grab an object to take up the air space and clench the fist tightly. Notice how much more solid the fist has become and how the "give" has been eliminated? A large chess piece, if smooth, will do. It doesn't have to be a roll of quarters. This same principle is used by professional boxers when they tape their hands before a fight: otherwise they might wind up with a broken hand even inside a padded glove.

If nothing is immediately available to slip into the palm the handroll can be used. Fold the fingers over as tightly as possible. The fingernails should dig into the thick meaty portion of the hand between the palm and knuckle joint. Keep the fingers as tight and close together as possible. Continue to roll the hand into a complete fist. The fingers will hurt a little bit and feel somewhat stiff and unnatural but there will be no looseness of the fist and your bones won't get crushed in the usual fashion if you land a haymaker on someone.

19

Be careful with this and check your victim over after he hits the ground. It isn't that hard to knock someone into a seizure. If your victim goes into convulsions and starts swallowing his tongue you had better be well versed in first aid or awful sure there are no witnesses. In some cases people can take unbelievable amounts of punishment and in others they die when you least expect it.

The Weapon Nobody Uses

Most normal, healthy adults in this day and age have a set of weapons they carry around with them that are almost as good as a knife at close quarters and yet never think to use them. Even in a life or death situation.

Those weapons are your teeth.

Don't think so? Just bite yourself a little bit. Anywhere you can reach with your own teeth will do. Notice the pain? See if your're man enough to draw blood on yourself. Now imagine what it would be like if someone else had a large chunk of you, muscle and all, in his mouth.

In wrestling around the bite, if a good healthy chunk on your opponent is latched on to, does two things:

1. It keeps you from getting hurt. A man can't hit you when you have your teeth buried in him. He can't hit you in your most vulnerable areas: eyes, nose, mouth, jaw, and neck. If he does hit you the blows will probably be gentle taps. Common sense has to tell him that a hard blow that goes wrong is subject to leave him missing a large chunk of his own body, the instantaneous removal of which is dreadfully painful.

2. It quite often paralyzes your opponent. In some cases it takes the heart completely out of them. Some men actually get to screaming. Others will hold your head almost like a caress. If you hold your bite is such a situation you then have time for a breather, to think out your next move, or whatever it is you want to do. As long as you hold your bite he will freeze. There are exceptions to this but they are so few and far between it isn't something you should be concerned with. It takes an awful lot of man to give up a chunk

of his body and take a chance of being scarred for life when all he has to do is say, "you win," "I give," or "I quit."

Jenks has used his teeth more than once. In one incident in Chillicothe prison in Ohio he found himself face down in the rain with his arms wedged into a curb and the man he was fighting was sitting on top of him. It looked like he didn't have a chance. His nose and mouth were under water and he thought he was drowning. His opponent got one of his fingers in Jenks' face, Jenks bit, and the finger came off completely at the first joint. The shock was enough to cause the other man to draw back just enough for Jenks to get an arm loose and put out one of the other man's eyes. End of fight.

Human bones are extremely strong but they are also extremely brittle. People's fingers snap about as readily as a chicken bone if you bite hard enough: and it doesn't have to be that hard. If you have false teeth, be careful. Real ones are about 100 times stronger.

If you know you have complete control of the situation even without a mouthful of flesh the option of gnawing is available. There is always something to bite on at close quarters. Gnawing will practically always get the other man to wiggling and in many cases will even cause him to beg for mercy. To get an idea of how it feels have someone pinch you on a fleshy part of the body using his thumb and at least two fingers. Now let him squeeze and pull. Hurts, doesn't it?

There are a few basics to keep in mind.

If you don't sink the eye teeth in up to the hilt then you're subject to come away with only a small morsel and and maybe even lose control of the situation. It's not the time to be dainty. The first weapons man ever had for close quarters were his teeth and the other man's instincts may take over if you blow it.

If you're wrestling and all locked up then it's time to bite. Obviously it's not going to work if you're circling and throwing blows from a range of two or three feet. If you wind up on the bottom of what is sometimes referred to as a "pig pile" it is literally possible to gnaw your way

22

out. Bite someone on the Achilles tendon, the one behind your heel, and it will snap and roll up like a rubber band. Most folks will leave the pile upon becoming hamstrung.

A lot of men might get sick to their stomach at the idea of swallowing large chunks of raw flesh off another human being or even at the thought of having it in their mouth. If the situation is serious enough all that should be going through your mind is thoughts of inflicting pain and winning. You can worry about looking like Vinnie the Vampire, blood coming from between your teeth and all, when the fight is over.

If someone else gets his teeth sunk in you any defense

Teeth are a very effective weapon, especially when used on tender fleshy areas.

must be done quickly. Go for his eyes. Try to inflict enough pain to get him to turn his head or loosen his jaws just long enough for you to get loose. You won't have much time as his hands will be just as free as yours once you make your move. If you try to pry his jaws open all he will wind up doing is biting harder. If you feel a slight slackening of pressure: jerk out.

Taking care of your teeth may preserve your health in ways your dentist never even dreamed of.

Historical Note: In the summer of 1978 a full-grown man attempted to rape a 14 year old girl in a parking lot in Lexington, Kentucky. He was armed with a knife. She obligingly pulled his pants down, acted like she was going to give him a blow job, and bit off a piece of his dipstick. The pain and shock were so intense and so unexpected he bolted from the scene without any attempt at retaliation. Lexington police later retrieved a small portion of the would-be rapists' anatomy from the scene and duly entered it as "evidence."

Several years before a man named Ballinger and his son raped and murdered several women and teen-age girls in the New Jersey/Pennsylvania area. Ballinger's last victim, also a 14 year old girl who refused to commit the same act and was subsequently stabbed to death and raped anyway.

Using her teeth more than likely would have saved her. Ballinger's son was a skinny 13 year old; it wasn't as if Ballinger had a "back-up" man to get even for him.

The Pad Lock

No judge or jury will send you to the pound these days for carrying a padlock around since thievery has become so common. It is just as effective as many saps, clubs, and the like if used properly. Just be sure you have a key to fit it or a combination to open it if you ever do get caught clobbering somebody with one.

To weild it as a weapon insert the middle finger through the U-shaped section of the lock and curl the finger around it by bending the middle finger at the first joint past the knuckle. There are two reasons for holding the lock in this fashion. First, the middle finger is the strongest of the fingers which in turn means more power and leverage can be put behind the blow than by holding it anywhere else. Second, by using the first joint past the knuckle of that finger the danger of the lock whipping back and smacking your own hand is minimized. Try a few practice swipes on a post with it and you'll catch our drift.

Almost any blow with a hand-held object consists of a cross-stroke and return. That is, if you hit from left to right then the next blow should be delivered right to left. Instantaneously.

The blow with the padlock would be delivered thusly:

1. Grab opponent's shirt or jacket with the left hand and pull him toward you to disturb his balance. A man off-balance usually can't hit hard enough to do any serious damage and normally can't use his strength or bodyweight to any advantage either. Simultaneously with yanking your opponent off balance draw the lock back into position and begin moving it in the direction of his jaw. The move must

be executed swiftly or you will be giving him time enough to get his hands up to protect his head.

2. As the lock travels inward twist the wrist in counterclockwise to assist in shifting your own bodyweight to get more power behind the blow and facilitate landing the blow squarely on the jaw-line. This is where left hooks or right crosses land most often in a prize fight and you'll notice such blows landed squarely often end those fights. Immediately.

3. Follow through. Don't just aim for the jaw, land the blow on it and then stop. If you've made the move properly the force of the blow, even on a direct hit, should carry the hand with the lock in it all the way across your own body.

4. In one smooth motion the lock should be brought back across the other man's face and returned to the original position. Whereas in move No. 2 the palm was facing up in the return move it should be facing toward the ground. The reason for this is simply that the hand will flip over naturally from the force of the blow and the momentum of your own bodyweight.

Again, don't forget your keys!

The proper grip on a padlock.

Padlock on a belt can be a lethal weapon.

LOCKS, SOCKS, AND STRINGS

A padlock can be used in a sock the same as bars of soap. However, there is a more effective use.

All that is required is a lock and a string, rope, or belt. A good strong leather shoelace does real well. Almost everyone wears belts, shoelaces, or both.

The principle is the same as that utilized by the weilder of the nun-chaku, a whipping motion.

Either wrapping it around the middle finger or swinging it at the end of a belt is very effective. Both methods are very efficient if used correctly.

Jenks got transferred out of Chillicothe prison in 1962 to Terre Haute and was then transferred to Leavenworth, Kansas. Jenks was put in a cell with eleven other men, only one of whom was friendly. The hostility started over the lack of personal hygiene practiced by the other men in the cell. Most of them worked in the kitchen or on the prison farm. The ones who worked on the farm, about ten of them, would come in with pig manure on their shoes, socks, and clothes. None of them took showers and would lay in the bunks and stink.

Jenks exchanged some serious words with them over their odor.

The only weapon Jenks had at the time was a padlock with a long shank.

There was one decent fellow in the cell and he and Jenks would play chess. Occasionally the chess game would go on for two, three, or four days in a row before either man won or lost. All the time Jenks and the ten other men in the cell were becoming less and less friendly.

Just before the hostilities erupted Jenks and his friend had been playing chess for two days. Things in the game were really getting interesting when the guards blew the whistle for supper one night. The chess game was left on a writing table that folded out from the wall.

When Jenks got back from supper the chess board was sitting upside down on his bed with all the chess men messed up. Jenks wound up in an argument with the other ten men over it and the man who was supposed to be the toughest in the cell jumped off his bed with the intention of attacking Jenks. Jenks had palmed his padlock and hit the tough guy before his feet touched the floor.

Jenks got a headlock on the other man and backed into a corner of the cell. Jenks had the lock around his middle finger and worked the tough guy over. Nine other men were trying to get to Jenks but they couldn't. Every time a man tried to get close Jenks would smack him with the lock. Every time the other men backed off Jenks would work over the tough guy. Every one in the cell got hit two or three times with the lock and Jenks never got hit once.

The fight didn't last very long. The guards ran up, broke up the fight, and took everyone to the hole. Jenks credits the lock with preventing him from being seriously hurt and allowing him to keep nine men off him without being hurt himself. He wasn't free to fight whole-heartedly and still managed to do serious damage to the man who started the whole affair.

A man with a lock on a belt or a string is sometimes more than a match for another man armed with a knife. In one instance in Terre Haute prison we observed one man armed with a knife back completely down from another man armed with a padlock and a shoelace. The man with the knife had started the trouble.

Photo taken at 1/500th of a second, showing the quickness and possible deadly results. (lock and belt are just a blurr)

Razor Blades & Toothbrushs

In a prison the convicts locked up on the "hole" or disciplinary segregation are normally not allowed razor blades. If they want to shave the guard has to stand and watch.

There are two reasons for this.

The first is that the "hole" is where all the trouble-makers are sent if that many people, sometimes over a hundred, with a penchant for causing trouble over and above the normal for a prison population are allowed any sort of cutting instrument on a regular basis lots of things besides whiskers are going to get cut.

The second is that a razor blade, a plastic toothbrush, and a book of matches are all that is necessary to make a small knife.

The brush end of the toothbrush is partially melted with a match, the razor blade inserted into the hot melted plastic, and the device then allowed to cool.

Such a weapon will usually serve to dissuade the other fellow from attacking since almost everyone has an instinctual fear of getting sliced to ribbons.

However, a razor cut or cuts will not usually stop people from fighting since the wounds are not felt. It's basically a "you've got me cornered now come and get me" type of weapon.

The Eyes Have It

One of the most effective moves to win a fight before it gets started is to simply jam the index and middle fingers of one hand into the other man's eyes. Whereas almost any sort of a telling blow requires balance to deliver, this one requires none. It takes so little power, an average-sized girl can incapacitate a 6' 200 lb. man with it very easily. It is especially useful when there isn't time to throw a punch.

The best way to make the move is to bring the hand to be used up like the mouth is going to be wiped in a nervous gesture and then strike. Any move to bring the hand into position close to the other man's eyes without alerting him.

Once you connect the fight is ended. Period. The chances of not connecting are very slim. Normally what happens is the blood vessels in the eyes are broken and will often take a month to heal.

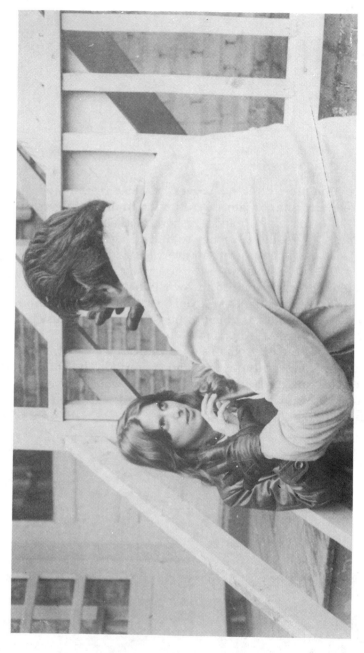

Seemingly helpless victim, but note position of right hand.

Driving fingers into attackers eyes, leaves him blind and now helpless.

37

Elbow Room

You've probably seen the bar-room brawls in the movies where someone pulls someone else's head down to waist level and then comes up with a knee lift to the face.

It's an excellent way to put yourself on crutches.

The kneecap is just about the easiest part of the body to shatter or dislocate. Jenks tried it a couple of times and wound up with a knee joint the size of a pumpkin.

The elbows and upper forearm are a different story. At close range, even at a distance of six inches, you can put everything you've got into a blow with an elbow. Every ounce of bodyweight can be used to deliver the blow. When there is no room to draw back or no time then the use of the elbows should be automatic, you should just fall into it. At short range using the entire arm length dissipates your power.

Try a few practice blows on a heavy punching bag from six inches away with your elbows, use the heavy muscles of the upper back to deliver the blow, and we believe you'll understand what we mean.

Photo on next page, shows the use of the elbow in close quarters.

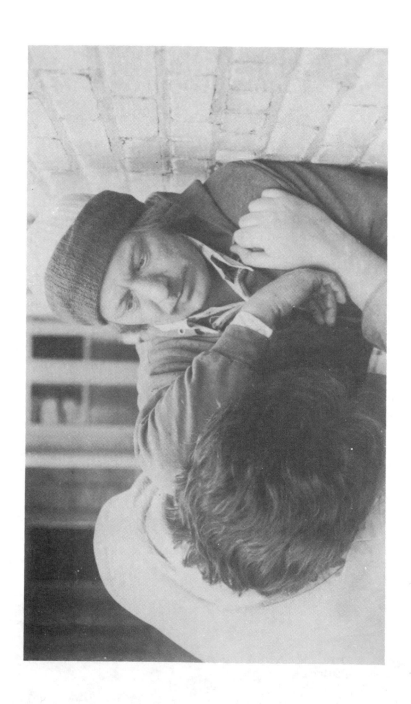

Ladies Hair Spray

This can be used two ways. If this sort of weapon appeals to you, you better stock up before all the "save the ozone" people get it removed from the market.

First is as a blinder. One good squirt in someone's eyes and they won't be able to see for awhile. In that respect it works as well as the little cans of Mace the market is glutted with and is far more functional.

The second is as a flame thrower. By holding a flaming lighter underneath the nozzle and depressing it the chemicals in the hair spray will ignite upon passing through the flame and often shoot fire for several feet.

This will also work with other aerosol spray cans such as paint. Ideally you would need a couple of minutes to get your lighter out and position the spray can so you don't shoot yourself in the face. For someone riding "shotgun" in a passenger car it's an ideal insurance policy to carry while cruising rough neighborhoods.

The homemade flame thrower can also be used for burning out spiders and wasps, even though this isn't a book on bug control.

Armed with a can of hairspray and a cigarette lighter . . . .

. . . . she is ready for the attacker with improvised flame
thrower.

Ballpoint Pens

Practically everyone these days carries a ballpoint pen. Properly held and properly thrust it can often put a man down or take the fight out of him quicker than a knife.

Before you use it you should understand that you are going to cause yourself some pain, injury, or discomfort when you use it. It is going to hurt. However, not anywhere near as much as it is going to hurt whoever you use it on. It's like taking a little to give a lot. You will definitely feel the pain.

The round end of the pen is butted against the heel of the palm and the sharp end thrust into the victim. An abdominal shot is usually the most effective. A man stuck in the liver or through the stomach will drop almost immediately.

Jenks first saw this used in isolation at Leavenworth. All the convicts had were a deck of cards, writing paper and envelopes, clothes with no belts, no shoes, and pencils.

The first time it happened a white man ran a pencil into the stomach of a black, about five or six inches. It was about an 8" pencil. The black had a serious injury and folded. Immediately.

The next day a fight erupted between four blacks and two whites. The blacks had the pencils. They got one white in the shoulder and the other one in the back. It was effective enough to win the fight. The whites didn't drop but it did take all the fight out of them, the only thing they were interested in was protecting themselves by dodging punches. The mental effect is the same as if you had an arrow sticking

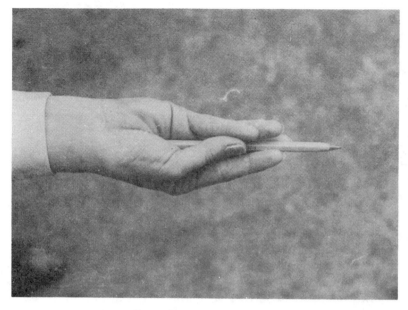

Correct grip for thrusting.

out of you. You could probably pull it out and go on about your business but it would take a much stronger stomach than the average man has.

Once you pulled it out, if you had the heart, you could probably keep fighting as effectively as before. We are, of course, not referring to a pen or pencil stuck in a vital organ.

The real problems develop later. One of the most serious wounds you can get is a puncture. Punctures are extremely hard to clean. A wound five inches deep and three inches long that is laid open you can clean but a wound five inches deep and 1/8 of an inch around, how do you get to the bottom to clean it?

Which means the chance of such a wound becoming infected are much greater than a normal open cut.

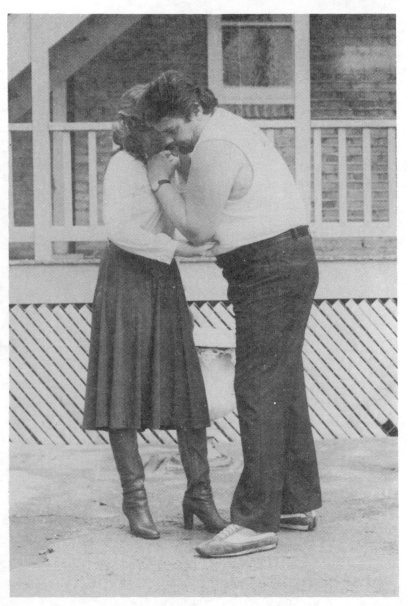

Pen being driven into attacker's stomach.

Drinking Glasses

The first thing that has to be understood about this weapon is that it is potentially harmful to the user. Extremely so. When glass breaks and cuts it cuts anything it can. His face. Your hand. Anything. If the move is made wrong there are going to be two people hurt instead of one and the second one will be yourself.

The heavy glass bottom of the glass is placed flat against the palm. The fingers are used to guide it. Above all you don't want your fingers wrapped around the glass when it shatters because if they are the glass will cut every single one of them. Badly.

The glass bottom would be the last part of the glass to break because it's the heaviest and strongest. Anytime it breaks it does so into the biggest pieces. Used in this fashion it seldom breaks.

The blow is delivered just like you intended to put the heel of your hand is someone's face. The difference is that you have the bottom of the glass against your palm and the lip of the glass connects with the other man's face. Just before the glass hits you have to spread your fingers way away from the glass and let the momentum stabilize in midair. Keep your fingers curled around the glass and you'll be cut on the hand as badly as your foe on the face.

Such a blow normally takes the fight out of folks. They will try to get away. Most people don't understand cuts and will try to get away to assess the damage.

The face and head are the best targets for this weapon. Hit someone on the chest or the stomach and the glass may not break. Nail a bony surface on the head and there will be cuts and blood everywhere.

Again a seemingly helpless victim, armed with only a drinking glass.

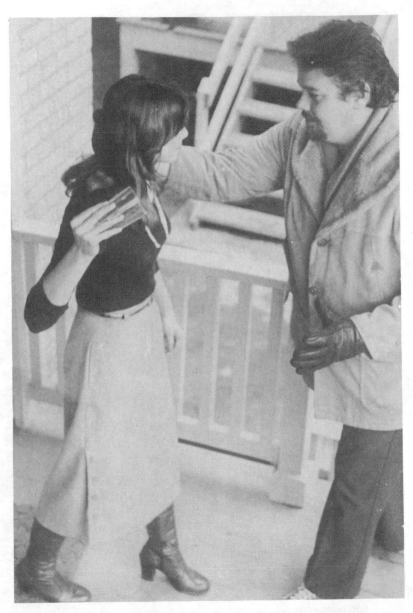

Victim shows proper grip and cocking for blow.

Driving glass into boney facial areas will result in glass shattering and serious cuts being inflicted on attacker.

Shoe Polish

Very few people would ever suspect how to use this weapon unless they could relate to what boiling oil was used for in the days of the Crusades. You've probably seen the knights-in-sardine-can movies where the rabble are repulsed by buckets of boiling oil poured on their head as they swarm up the siege ladders to the castle.

In prison it's usually the only available weapon of that nature. Anyone who has spit-shined shoes knows the principles of melting the wax to get a better shine. Let the flame burn for two to three minutes and the shoe polish becomes very, very hot, just like hot pitch.

Jenks used it once at Chillicothe.

He had just gotten out of the hole. At the time he was 19 years old and had, on the starvation diet forced on him in the hole, lost so much weight he could hardly walk. From a height of 6'8" and a weight of 285 the prison hacks had starved him down to 147.

When he got out of the hole he was living in a single cell on the upper range. Some trouble had developed between Jenks and five other men and they had let him know they were going to "get" him the next morning.

The bottom cells were opened first the next morning and the five started hollering up at Jenks. He knew that when the guards opened his door all five were going to swarm on him. If he fought them he knew that win, lose, or draw he was going to be badly hurt.

The cell doors at Chillicothe were solid iron, there were no bars to see through.

Jenks wrapped a piece of wire around a can of shoe polish and lit it. Jenks was sitting on a locker with the blazing shoe polish in his hand when the five trouble-makers tried to crowd in. As soon as they saw the flames they turned and ran. Jenks nailed the last one on the back. Had they kept coming the first one would have gotten it in the face. As it was the hot shoe polish splattered everywhere.

Put your finger in hot tar or hot pitch that the county road crews resurface the streets with and you'll get an idea of how painful it is.

Just don't expect it to keep burning after you throw it. The fire goes out with any sudden motion. Again, it's like hot pitch.

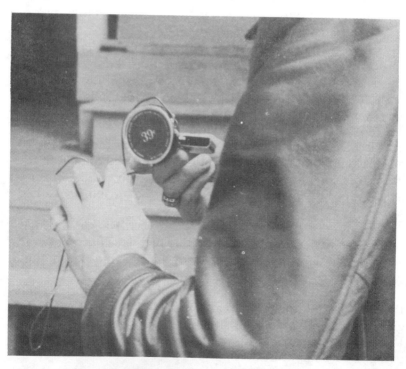

Preparing shoe polish for weapon.

This same principle can be used with boiling water or hot food on a stove. Grease in a cooking skillet is especially effective since it retains its heat a lot longer than shoe polish. It's almost guaranteed that a man with a knife is going to back off from a woman with a boiling pot in her hands and it's a sure cure for peeping toms or burglars trying to get in a window. A snootful of boiling food in the face will send them home everytime.

A burning cigarette stuck in someone's ear will work much in the same fashion. You just have to get closer.

When lit, shoe polish liquefies and becomes a very serious weapon.

Ash Trays

The ash tray can be used in two basic ways.

One is to simply grab it by the rim and flail away with the corners. The best ash tray for our purposes is one of the heavy glass ones sold in stores everywhere, square on the top and round on the bottom.

The other is a parallel to the suriken used by the medieval Japanese, a star-shaped piece of metal flung like a frisbee at a pursuer.

The ash tray should be hurled like a frisbee. Underhanded, overhanded, with a flip of the wrist from left to right using the right hand and the muscles of the upper back, it makes no difference. As long as plenty of "spin" is imparted to the ash tray it will work. Throwing it end over end won't work.

Hit somebody in the head like this and it will look like someone worked him over with an axe, sinking in up to four or five inches in the skull. A small girl can drop a full-grown man with it. Provided of course, she knows how to throw. A lot of women can't throw a football the length of a baby bed and if they a throw a bowie knife they're not going to do any damage either.

Hit a man in the rib cage with a flying, spinning ash tray and it will do more damage than a set of brass knuckles simply because of the velocity and momentum.

If the ash tray, if it's a big glass one, hits a wall or the floor it will usually break. If it hits a person first it won't break until after it has hit, done the damage, and bounced to the floor.

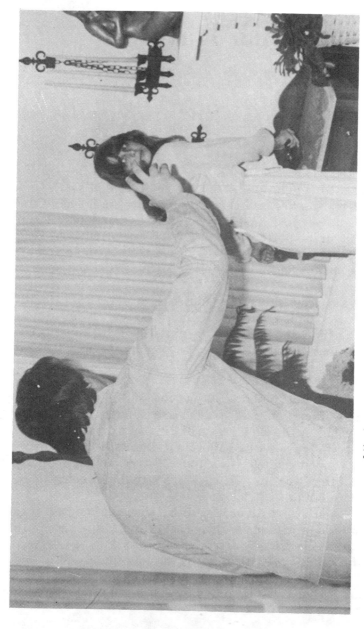

Attacker approaching, (note the ashtray she's grabbing).

Victim driving corner of ashtray into attacker's throat.

Correct grasp on ashtray for throwing at attacker.

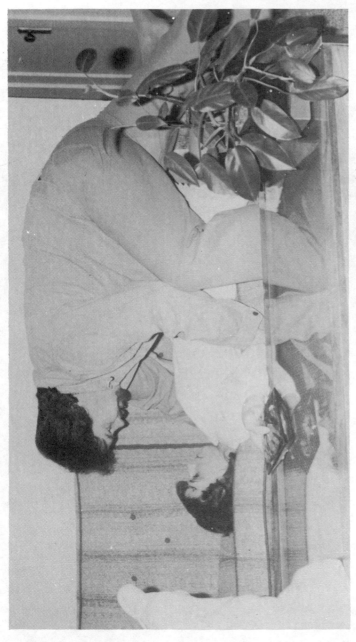

Here victim is trapped, but can still reach ashtray. By driving a corner into the side of the attacker's head (temple area), she would be freed.

Whiplash

This was a favorite back in the 1950's. It's the old "crack-the-whip" principle that has been around for centuries. Get any object moving fast enough and when it hits, it hurts.

The same principle can be used with a clothes hanger, a fishing pole, a bullwhip, or anything similar.

And if you don't believe it hurts, have someone do it to you.

The pain is excruciating.

Up Against The Wall

Most normal people don't think of a wall as a weapon. It's not something you pick up and clobber something with. Even Samson, the best he could do was a set of city gates.

Like the old bromide goes, if the mountain won't go to Mohammed then Mohammed should go to the mountain.

Ever notice how a lot of men, especially in prison, will stand with one hand braced on the wall over a urinal?

The reason is that grabbing someone's head like a big piece of fruit and smashing it against a wall or a bar top is very, very effective. It's the same as hitting them with a cement club, only with less velocity.

Brass Knuckles

You may have seen the magazine ads for "knucks." An apparently flat sand casting of aluminum with holes for the fingers and a brace for the palm of the hand.

And if you've ever used them without prior instruction in their use you either broke your fingers or hit something very soft.

The ones in the magazines are not made by the people who ever had any real-life experiences with brass knuckles. They can be used, are a definite improvement over the bare fist, are easily concealable, and are relatively cheap.

Breaking your fingers is a heavy price to pay to get one good punch in. Especially if you're fighting two or three people at the same time.

Let's start with carrying the weapon.

There are several different places that a flat pair of knucks, the kind you see advertised in SOLDIER OF FORTUNE magazine and elsewhere, can be carried. Most of them are wrong.

The back pocket is an obvious place to carry a set. And a good way to put yourself into a very bad position while starting a fight. The first disadvantage you have is that you have to put one hand behind you to pull them out. Which means you have only one arm free to defend yourself if the other man decides to swarm you. The second disadvantage is that your opponent immediately knows you're going for a weapon and will conduct himself accordingly. You're giving him too much warning. If he runs, well and good. If he thinks you're coming out with a gun and has one of his own you stand a better than average chance of getting ventilated.

The front pocket isn't any better. Same basic problem.

The proper place to carry a set of knucks is behind the belt line. That way no-one knows what your intentions are in time enough to react. Just any place behind the belt line won't do.

Photo No. 1 shows the proper way to carry them. A right-handed man, such as the one in the photo, carries them on his left side behind and slightly below the belt. Normally a slight pressure from the bottom half of the belt will hold them in place but you could go to a little holster if you feel insecure. It might be a little embarrassing if they got loose and clattered to the floor in the local supermarket. Notice how his elbow is close in to the body. A good section of his torso is protected. The move could very easily be mis-interpreted as a protective one since the hand is coming up from the side and placed over the mid-section: meaning the other fellow doesn't know you're going for a weapon until it's too late. Notice how the man in the photo has his right index finger hooked into the first hold on the knucks and is pulling upwards.

In photo No. 2 notice how easily the second and third fingers fall right into place as the weapon is pulled up and forward. The entire sequence should be a natural flowing movement.

As the knucks clear the belt the top part of the hand, the thumb and index finger section, should be tilted forward just enough to allow the weapon to slide from the first to the sec-ond joint of the fingers simply because of its own weight in relation to gravity. This is illustrated in photo No. 3. Practice this a few times and you will see how easy and natural it feels.

In photo No. 4 our man is in position and moving. Don't let the still-life position of the photos confuse you. The entire move, from slipping the index finger into the first hole on the knuck to connecting with someone's head, should take less than a second. The other man shouldn't know you had a set of knucks until AFTER he has been hit with them. In the photo the move being made is a semi-circular one, not straight-on as would first appear. The idea is to shift the

Photo No. 1

Photo No. 2

Photo No. 3

bodyweight from right to left and swing the arm and hand around to transfer the bodyweight shift to the blow. It can't be done straight on. The left hand is on the collar of the other man's jacket for two reasons. The first and most important is that it allows him to pull the other man forward and control him, keeping him off balance. A man off balance normally cannot swing hard enough to do any damage. The second is that you simply cannot afford to have an arm or hand "hanging back" from the fight. In the photo our man has not only pulled his opponent off-balance but also has his left arm positioned in such a fashion it is almost impossible for his victim to get in a "head shot."

In photo No. 5 the blow is depicted. Notice how the hand is at right angles to the body from moving the hand and arm in a semi-circular motion described earlier. This is a raking, not a punching motion. There are a couple of words of caution in order at this point.

One is that the knucks on the market today, weren't designed for a raking movement. They are too big. Someone DID intend to use them for punching and simply didn't know what he was doing when he made them. Ditto for everybody else that copied him. We are simply explaining the only feasible way to use a very ill-designed piece of equipment. More on this later.

The other is that you had better determine how much damage you want to inflict before you start. If you want to kill a man it's not hard. Hit him high on the side of the head and you stand a good chance of having it sink in just like it would on a mush melon having the other fellow's brains dribbling out on your hand. Hit him about eye level and you may take an eye out. Hit him anywhere below that level and you have a really good chance of getting away with a light or suspended sentence if and when it goes to court. The worst that can happen is he'll lose some teeth, you'll break his jaw, his nose will be moved over to the other side of his face, or you'll crush his cheekbone. Which normally should be enough to take all the fight out of him.

In photo No. 6 the force of the blow carries the weapon past the victim's head as the semi-circular arc continues.

In photo No. 7 the blow has been carried to completion. That is, the blow from right to left. The principle here is the same one we wrote of in BLOODY IRON, our book on knife fighting. There is no room for wasted motion. If you make a move from right to left you must immediately use the force of the recoil, whether it be a slash with a knife or a raking motion with a set of knucks, to move back in the original direction. Again note how the knucks are positioned on the fingers.

In photo No. 8 the man with the knucks is moving back from left to right. Even if he missed the first time he may catch his opponent on the backswing. If he connected badly the first time and merely stunned the other man the second blow should be enough to drop him.

Somewhere along here you have to make a value judgment. And it has to be made quickly. Photo No. 9 illustrates this. If you can feel the man go limp through the hold you have on his jacket you can probably let him drop and you will have no further problems with him on that particular day. If he keeps struggling you will have to determine whether he just wants to get away or is still full of fight. If he merely wants to run let him go: unless he has a gun in his car or something he's trying to get to. If he still has plenty of fight left in him then you had better be able to think quickly. You don't want to get hurt yourself and neither do you want the knucks sinking into his head like a piece of iron into over-ripe fruit. Especially in front of witnesses. Best bet is probably to just keep raking him across the face until your left arm and hand transmit the feeling of limpness normally associated with unconsciousness.

If you're really fortunate, know the right people, have a reputation for keeping your mouth shut, and a goodly supply of money, someone may offer to sell you a set of professional brass knuckles. They're called "pros" and come in two parts, the "pros" and the "knockers." Normally you have to be what the underworld refers to as "on the muscle" to even come across such equipment. That is, an extortionist or someone who gets paid a tremendous amount of money for teaching people manners or encouraging them

71

Photo No. 4

Photo No. 5

73

Photo No. 6

Photo No. 7

Photo No. 9

to pay their bills on time. Even in or among the criminal element or loan-sharking profession most of the participants never heard of them.

Both together are referred to as a "set of pros." It's a confusing terminology. The pros are very light, very thin, with little sharp points, that fit over the middle joint of the fingers. The thickness is about that of a comb. It's a tight fit. They are for close-in work. Used for raking.

The knockers are the ones used for punching. They are big, bulky, and very hard to conceal. Both are usually made out of aluminum simply because of the weight factor. Knockers ride high on the hand and cover the knuckles. Even though they are referred to as a "set" they are not worn on the same hand at the same time. An analogy would be the old 19th century .44-40: you could use the cartridge in a set of weapons, rifle and pistol, for different purposes.

Using the pros is just like planting a field, like making furrows. The difference between pros and a plow is that the plow makes the furrows in a field and the pros make them in someone's face. If you want to make the other man look like the lead villain in a Vincent Price movie you use pros. Hit someone with knockers and things will break. Rake them with pros and things will cut. The cuts or grooves applied with such a weapon leave wounds of a fashion that no plastic surgeon can straighten them out. It's a good way to mark a man for life and a man faced with the prospect of getting worked over with a set would do well to reconsider coming to some kind of an agreement with the people he's doing business with. It's an extremely cruel and vicious piece of equipment.

There's a large difference in what happens legally if someone gets caught with a set of pros before the event as opposed to being nailed during or after the act. Before most law enforcement officers would merely slap a "carrying a concealed weapons" charge on the owner and that would be the end of it. To them it would be just another set of knucks.

Get nailed in the act or afterwards and it's not so simple. Most States have statutes that separate "maiming" from "assault with a deadly weapon." Assault charges normally carry from a year or less to ten years, very seldom any more.

Maiming often carries life imprisonment. It is often put in the same class as torture or castration.

The knucks for sale through the magazines differ from pros in several respects. Some of the ones sold through the magazines have points on them just like the pros. Not a set of pros, just the pros. The ones in our photos are something like pros except that they are two or three times too large. And two or three times too thick. The ones in our photos are off-set. That is, the ring for the middle knuckle is higher than the others and so on. Pros are flat straight across. Commercial models, like the one our model is using, have a brace for the palm of the hand. Pros don't have any. Pros are flat, as opposed to offset, on both sides.

Knockers are offset. If you make a fist and hold it where you can see the knuckles and the back of the hand but not the fingers you'll get an idea of what we mean. The knockers cover the knuckles and middle joint of the fingers without touching them. An S-shaped piece of metal holds the striking surface in place and butts against the hand. The idea is that when the blow is landed all the pressure is taken up in the palm of the hand, there is simply no pressure on the knuckles. This concept probably originated in the Middle Ages with the armored steel glove of the knights. If you go to a museum that has suits of armor some of the gloves will have spikes sticking out of them. With no brace behind the spikes the knight would be just as liable to break his own fingers as he would anything else on an adversary. Keep the spikes from contact with the knuckles by the use of an S-shaped brace in the palm and putting some serious dents in the other man's helmet became a definite option at close quarters. Not to mention the S-shaped piece of metal made holding a mace, battle-axe, or sword somewhat less difficult. The armored gloves may not have always had an S-shaped brace but they almost always did have a brace of some kind. Anything else would have resulted in broken fingers.

Properly put together a pair of knockers will allow you to punch a concrete wall just as hard as your speed and body-weight will allow. It's not likely you would run into a man wearing a steel helmet but they do an excellent job of caving a man's ribs in without skinning the knuckles of the user.

There have been sets of knucks made to cover only two or three fingers, from the index finger on down. Why anyone would use such a set is a mystery to us and a practice we do not recommend.

Our original set of pros came out of New York City many, many years ago. The pros fit like a glove with no room in the fingers. The knockers were big and bulky, like something a bartender would keep behind the bar for arguments with obnoxious customers.

Unfortunately, a fellow who shall hereinafter remain nameless dropped the only set of pros we had access to into a river outside of Chattanooga, Tennessee. Which made taking photographs of them impossible.

If you really wanted to you could probably get a set made or even make them yourself with a method of metal-working that's been around since the Egyptians, called lost wax casting. Having someone else do it could get pretty expensive.

If you want a set of pros to hang on the wall as a conversation piece it might be worth the expense. Use them on someone in a streetfight and some judge may decide to hang YOU on the wall. There are situations where such weapons are necessary but you had better be aware of the consequences before you use them.

One particular judge told us that a pair of knucks is strictly an offensive weapon, whereas a pistol can be used offensively or defensively. The law definitely frowns on knucks. The "strictly offensive" business may be far from accurate if six people have you backed into an alley and you drop one or two of them getting away but it's usually the way the courts and the police look at it. You can bet if you go to court the same six people will claim you started it for a reason. In this day and age the folks who win the courts cases are not necessarily the ones in the right. Most often they are those who can lie the best.

Which means you had better have a GOOD story if you get caught using them. It may not be good enough to convince a police officer or a judge of your innocence but if the D.A. thinks you will totally confuse the jury the whole case

has a good chance of being thrown out.
Unless you kill somebody.
Be careful.

KNOWLEDGE

The Most Invisible of All

Weapons

Things in a United States prison are far different than what you see on the glass toilet, read in books, or just naturally assume. For example, it is naturally assumed that the guards and other prison personnel run the prison. It seems logical. However, the prisoners actually run the prison: this contention is borne out of every time the prisoners go "on strike." Normally, prisoners run the prison industry, the repair shops, and take care of any paperwork that needs doing. In a strike everything shuts down.

In Lewisburg in 1975 the convicts struck. I was working in the machine shop at the time and looked out the window to see several hundred convicts milling in the yard. Since it was my first year in the joint I immediately misinterpreted what was going on and went for a weapon. The machine shop was full of them — heavy iron bars, sharpened pieces of metal, a few shanks (homemade knives), and an occasional real lulu: like the .38 caliber revolver three convicts had cranked out in the machine shop the week before and then destroyed when they realized they would never make a parole if they were caught with it. One tall slender colored fellow who ran the planer did lose his parole date because of what he did in our shop. He was making counterfeit plates for various denominations of federal reserve notes.

About the time I found a satisfactory length of iron pipe other convicts came running in the shop yelling "strike" and I put down my iron. I thought a riot was, in prison parlance, "jumping off." Within seconds the loudspeakers blared for all prisoners to return to their housing units.

As we walked back to our cells, I could see the guards were edgy. I don't blame them. If the convicts decide to "go off" on them they didn't have a chance. There were hundreds of us. There were, at best, a few dozen of them. Many of us were armed. None of them were. A few guards in the towers surrounding the prison had carbines and shotguns but they were of little use to their fellow officers: their field of vision was limited to the prison wall and the yard. Anything that happened inside was going to be done with before they had a chance to react.

When I got back to my cell the only thing on my mind was that I now had the afternoon off, I could curl up with a good book, and they would call us for chow like they always did; which in Lewisburg consisted of a couple of toots on a whistle.

But the guards were more nervous than I thought. They came and got us cellblock by cellblock to eat. That is, there were eighteen (18) men in my block (I was in "A" block, maximum security, which had a much smaller population than the other cellblocks) and we were taken to the mess hall in a group, ate in a group, left in a group, and after we were locked back up the next cellblock was let out to eat. Some cellblocks didn't get fed until almost midnight. Normally, cellblocks are let out to eat at ten-minute intervals. And normally feeding the entire captive population of over 1500 men takes less than two hours. This time it took six. Of course, pulling the industry supervisors and guards out of the prison industry and making them wash our dirty dishes and trays didn't speed things up any.

Shortly after the strike I was approached by another convict who locked next to me on "A" block. He asked me if I wanted to buy a .38 Special with a box of shells for "400 green" ("green money" in the federal system is distinguished

84

from money you can have "on the books" for commissary, it means cash and is contraband inside the walls). I laughed in his face. If I needed a gun I could have one made in the machine shop but nobody could convince me that Smith & Wessons and Colts with boxes of ammunition floated around inside the prison compound.

A week later the whole prison administration was in an uproar. A colored guard walked into the prison and put what appeared to be his lunch, in a paper sack, on another officer's desk. Someone called the colored guard over the loudspeaker and asked him to move his car as he had parked it in a no-parking zone in front of the prison. He went out to move his car and left his "lunch" on the table. The other officer picked up the paper sack to move it off some of his papers. Wondering why a sack lunch would weigh six pounds, he looked inside. What he saw was a .38 Smith & Wesson with a box of bullets.

Two inmates were finally found to snitch on the guard. However, the men he was "doing business" with were "stand-up" and wouldn't squeal under any circumstances and so what the government wound up with was a case consisting of hearsay, not enough for a criminal conviction. The guard lost his job.

What I hadn't realized at the time was that the convict offering me the gun for "400 green" was trying to do me a favor; that was what the guard was charging for them. As close as I could determine about two dozen revolvers had been sold inside the wall and hidden in various places by the purchasers. For reasons known only to himself the colored guard sold his guns only to the white prisoners. One of them, a fellow named McCoy doing 45 years for airplane hijacking, evidently used his purchase to commandeer a garbage truck (with the help of two other prisoners), peg a couple rounds at the tower guard, and run through the front gate in August 1974. Unfortunately, McCoy learned the hard way what most prisoners know instinctively: getting out of prison is no problem, it's keeping your act together once you get out. McCoy walked into his apartment in Virginia Beach, Virginia less than six months later with a sack full of groceries in his arms. He never got to eat them. An FBI agent lurking inside his apartment shot him at point blank range with a 12-gauge shotgun; killing him instantly.

Not too long afterwards I was introduced to another couple of prisoner favorites in weapons. One was explosives. The other was fire.

Like most of your average citizens, I didn't think explosives were available to prisoners. Once in a while someone would set off a match-head pipe bomb or similar crude device but I never suspected anything sophiscated.

One prisoner had gotten extremely tired of other prisoners stealing his radio. He would engrave his prison number on it, take it with him to the gym, and invariably whenever he turned his back another inmate would run off with it. He decided to teach someone a lesson. He wired his newest radio with explosives and left it in the corner of the gym. He walked away from it. Someone picked it up and walked off with it. Whoever got it turned it on while he was walking down the stairs away from the gym and the charge went off. A pall of black smoke drifted back into the gym. Nice try, but the victim of the blast was a guard who had picked it up to return it to its owner.

By the time I was released three years later bombs in the compound had become so commonplace they were boring. An explosion the size of a hand grenade in the yard didn't even disturb the guards.

Fire in the prison was far more deadly. Referred to as "burn-outs," they usually took one of two forms. The first was to simply soak a cell with an inflammable liquid and set it to the match. This was a polite way of letting the cell occupant know that he was considered persona non grata by the other residents of the cellblock. A wise prisoner would then ask for a housing change. The second form of "burn-out" was usually far more serious. The idea was to kill the occupant. If the man was locked in his cell and a firebomb was thrown in, death was automatic. If the cell wasn't locked he still didn't have much of a chance since his killers would brace the door shut with a wedge-shaped piece of wood or the sides of their feet. Firebombs were easy to make, gasoline from the power lawnmowers and soap for the laundry was usually available.

Bombs, guns, and knives are obvious weapons to anyone. But prisoners often run in packs and operate like armies, which includes communications and intelligence. Sometimes with fatal results to federal employees.

In "A" block in 1975 I had an interesting conversation with a convict who had been shipped out to Leavenworth. He was "doing it all" (couldn't make a parole) off a five-year sentence about to get out. When I inquired as to his lack of parole eligibility he explained that, in a cell with seven other men, the guards found an FBI agent with his head severed from his body after the prisoners had left for "work call." To this day no one knows who did it. I got the rest of the story over two years later in Terre Haute from another cell member who had also been transferred out of Leavenworth.

What had happened was the FBI agent came in after the evening meal when all convicts were supposed to be off work. One convict in Receiving and Discharge wasn't (R & D is where prisoners are processed in or out). He saw the FBI agent turn in his gun, take off his badge, and put on prison khakis. The prisoner left R & D without being seen and communicated the facts to the convict population.

The agent walked into his death cell, went to the commode and defecated a plastic bag with green money in it, and offered to buy narcotics. No one offered to sell him any and the next morning he was dead.

Oral communication wasn't the only method the convicts used. An electronics wizard mentioned in "Watergate on the Wabash" in Penthouse magazine showed me how to take two radios, put them exactly on the same channel (I forget whether AM or FM but you can find out yourself in 30 seconds; I have only one radio in my house), and tap on the speaker with your finger of one of the radios. The tapping will be audible from the speaker of the other one. This individual was sent out to the prison farm (mostly snitches and rats) to keep him from teaching the rest of us what he knew. Not, however, before I got a schematic of a blue box and an excellent working knowledge of how to build and operate a red box. Our electronics genius was doing three years for one $9.11 phone call.

All the foregoing was simply what was available inside the prison. Other trinkets could be ordered. Some convicts in Atlanta had a 12-gauge sawed-off shotgun and a box of shells smuggled in inside a cake. In Arizona a man's sons broke him out at gunpoint. In Lewisburg I checked a book out of the prison library that gives specific instructions on smuggling things into the prison, including but not limited to sawing wooden chess pieces in half and secreting bullets in hollowed out sections and gluing them back together and mailing the chess set into the prison, sewing green money, narcotics, blades, and other goodies inside hardcover book bindings, and switching shoelaces containing gigli saws in the visiting room. A gigli saw is flexible and so slim it can be hidden inside a shoelace and so strong it is used to cut steel in half. The best "home delivery" I heard of came off but if it had the whole country would have seen it on TV and in the newspapers.

The idea was to have an outside accomplice fly a piper cub with a smoke attachment for the exhaust directly over the exercise yard. With the plane billowing smoke the tower guards would think the plane was going to crash directly into the prison and be running for lower ground. Nobody wants to be in a tower an airplane is about to crash into. Once the plane cleared the prison walls and was over the exercise yard the pilot was to kick out a bundle of pistols, gear to scale the walls, and whatever other goodies were obtainable (such as land anti-tank weapons, etc.). In the confusion and smoke the convicts would go over or through the walls. A similar operation took place in Terre Haute in a heavy fog one morning. 400 hundred men walked out to the prison industry to go to work and 18 of them just kept walking. Three of them had wire cutters in their pockets and simply cut their way through the chicken wire fence surrounding the prison. One of them walked half a mile to the Wabash river, plopped himself on a floating log, and had a leisurely breakfast in Louisville, Kentucky the next morning.

Two "weapons" more deadly and more invisible than all the others put together need mentioning. One is money. The other is the human mind. For enough money anyone — up to and including the warden — can be "taken out." At one time the Mafia ran Lewisburg by greasing the prison personnel and muscling the other convicts (who could they complain to?). I used to watch them kiss each other on the cheeks when a busload got shipped out (and almost had a heart attack when a guy at a mess hall table with me asked loud enough for everyone to hear, "are those guys queer?").

The human mind has to be the deadliest. With a gun, a knife, or a bomb your options are limited. There are only certain ways they can be used. Money is more flexible, but there are still limitations. Once a flap came up about letting certain types of books into the prisons — as if convicts couldn't acquire the information any other way. What nonsense. All the ACLU did in their court case regarding reading material was make a simple operation simpler. Any time any of us wanted a "forbidden" book we simply had someone on the outside take off the covers and replace them with something like "freshman geometry" or "English essay writing." A good many of the guards were functional illiterates and never checked anything but the covers anyway. Whatever it was we wanted, we could think of some way to get it. Some guys even got women into the prison, serviced them, and sent them on the way. Unfortunately, a warden caught two couples banging away in the Officer's Mess Kitchen one day (you have to be careful what the prisoners put in the food) and things got tightened up for awhile. I don't know how many copies of the CIA Black Books and other bomb books were circulating when I was in, but it was a bunch.

There seems to be some concern about the type of criminal who might get ahold of certain information. Most federal criminals are usually doing time for white collar crime, bank robbery, or large-scale narcotics operations, "thinking man's" crime that requires careful preparation and foresight. Besides which the FBI depends so heavily on informers (95% of their convictions are obtained through snitches) that all they salt away are the dumb, the careless (like myself), and the clumsy. The REAL crooks are not locked up. Your Congressman can buy any book he wants.

State criminals are somewhat more erratic but the really nasty ones are usually kept in isolation (where the materials for mayhem are simply not available) for their own protection. A child molester is likely to meet his end in general population for two reasons: he won't have any friends which in turn make him "prey" for any disgruntled convict with a knife. That doesn't happen with normal convicts. The last time a yo-yo in Terre Haute ran his mouth at a friend of mine three of us fell out of the yard to lend a hand — and at 6'2" and 220 lbs. I was the smallest of the three. The mouth runner never showed.

Why our state and local governments keep funding prison systems is a mystery to me. The horsewhip and the executioner would be cheaper and far more effective. What prisons do is accentuate, heighten, and sophiscate whatever mental qualities a man has — for good OR evil. Germany locked up a somewhat uncoordinated street agitator in Landsberg Prison in 1923 and in 1925 disgorged a real sophiscate: Adolf Hitler.

Is out next Hitler in our prisons? Or is he out and is it already too late?

An Interview With Jenks

On Hand-to-Hand Combat

Philosophy

How do people usually react when they are shot?

Let's say we're talking about a burglary. Someone breaks in your house. If you shoot him and he is a weak person, he might fall, but would he give up? Ninety percent of the time he would. But, if he was a strong individual, unless you really hit hard enough to put him down where he would have to fall, he wouldn't. That's up to an individual person. There are people who get shot in the arm and they'll cry and beg and fall down and never move. Then there are those people who you could shoot their head off and they're still going to try to get away or they're going to try to come back. It's a determination. It would be the same thing barehanded, there's guys you can hit one time and they'll fall down and cry. They're not real seriously hurt, or anything. They may not be hurt at all, other than they got hit and they give up and won't fight. And the next guy, you can beat him half to death but he's still going to get up and throw one more punch. The difference in those two types of people is the same difference that you would have with somebody getting shot or stabbed. It's up to the individual how much punish-

91

ment they will absorb before their heart breaks or before their courage breaks.

If they have a chance to prepare themselves — that's probably the most important thing. It would then be up to what the circumstances were and who they were with. In other words, a fellow who knows he's going to be in the jack pot is going to be a lot harder to deal with than the same guy if you just hit him broadside unexpectedly. His instincts will take over if you Pearl Harbor him, but if he knows that he's going to have problems he's a lot more subject to get himself geared up. You know in your own experiences where people who would normally not do anything out of the ordinary. You put a play together and you take them with you and you're either leading them or they're right beside you, they'll do things then that they would never normally do. They would absorb a lot more punishment than they would normally just because they're with you, it's expected and they know that that's what's going to happen where if they were on their own and somebody walked up and punched them in the nose they might not even fight.

What is it that causes a group to do what they or individuals would not do?

In a group the people that I know, there are friends of mine that are basically weak people; if they were with me and something came down they would be hard to handle because they would be with me. They wouldn't want to quit. The fear of getting hurt would be not near as great as the fear that they would have of everybody knowing they were a coward and knowing they gave up when they were with me and leaving me in the lurch because we're friends. That overrides. The fear of humiliation.

That fear overrides, it's the same thing like in the service. The service is made up of just regular people, most of them individually are not very strong, but as a unit they'll attack a hillside and half of them get killed. They'll go back the next day and attack it again and half of them again get killed. On an individual basis if you tried to get one of them to charge up that hill as a civilian or whatever there's no way they would ever do it. But as a unit and with their family and reputation behind them, court martial for cowardice in battle, and that kind of stuff the feeling they get with being part of a unit and being with their friends and buddies will make them go way above anything they would do as a normal individual. Which is why, during war time, a man will shoot people every day or shoot at people or fire a cannon every day that's going to kill people or drop a bomb that's going to kill people. You can live next door to that same individual and he probably wouldn't get in a fist fight. The difference is the circumstances that they're in and who they're with.

If you are facing a group the first determination you would have to make is whether or not the group has a leader. If a group has a recognized leader and the people who are following recognize him as a leader, then you have serious problems. But if you have a group of friends opposing you it's different. If you're facing fifteen people and there is no recognized leader, there is no organization, it's no club, or there's no recognized leader as such, then if one person is doing something you would have some that would want to stop him, some that would want to help him, and some that would not want any part of it.

The "peace marches" that were busted up in the 1960's weren't following a leader, see they were following a movement, which is a completely different thing. It would be if they had one leader. If it was the President of the United States that was charging down the middle of the street a lot of Americans would follow him because they recognize him as the leader, although they may not agree with what he's doing on this particular thing. They would follow him but it would be just like the leader of a bike club. If the president of a bike club is there and he says let's do this and if goes and does it everybody will follow him if he is in fact the leader and has the respect of the people behind him, they'll follow him. But if you get ten bikers together that don't have a leader, especially from different clubs, and one guy gets in it, there's no telling what the response of the rest of them is going to be. Some guys feel like getting into something and would go along with the program and some guys will say, you know we shouldn't do it, we don't need the trouble.

We're talking about something other than one individual deciding on what the same individual does. We're talking about outside influences, whether it be somebody else or the chance to prepare himself. I know guys that prepare themselves to box. I watch the fights on TV. They know what they're going to get into where you probably take the same guy in the street and he would not fight near as hard in the street as he would in the ring and another guy would fight five times harder on the street than he ever would in the ring. It's just different.

If you want to nail somebody, if you want to creep on somebody, then it would be best, especially if you think you're dealing with a weak individual, to get him by himself, not because you can whip him easier that way but because if he is with a stronger individual or a situation like I was just describing, you have monumental problems.

What is the most important thing to consider when it looks like trouble is going to start?

Probably the most important thing is deciding when something's going to be necessary. If I know without a doubt that you and I are going to have a fight, and I know that it may take us fifteen minutes of arguing or ten minutes of arguing or whatever, but I know in the end we're going to have serious problems. As soon as you decide that in your own mind, then that's the time to move. You don't wait for somebody else to get themselves prepared. If you're going to have trouble with somebody, or if you're running a business and you have somebody come in your business that's creating a disturbance and you've tried to talk to them, you know whether or not they're the type of person you're going to be able to talk out of it, talk into leaving, or handling it without a problem. But if in talking to them you decide that there is no way this guy is going to straighten up and there's no way this guy is going to leave or whatever you're trying to get him to do without having trouble with him, then the first thing you do is to do whatever you would do if it had already progressed that far. It's the practice of simply anticipating his moves. He knows there's going to be trouble, you know there's going to be trouble. Move in first. It's not a first punch. It's not a "Pearl Harbor" move. This is getting a guy that's relaxed and not expecting it. Pearl Harbor is like I want to have trouble with you. For some reason I want to whip you. You don't expect anything for whatever reason and I just walk up to you and knock your brains out. That's Pearl Harboring.

But when you have somebody who knows that they're doing something wrong and out of hand and you know that you're going to have trouble with them, then what you're merely talking about is who moves first. There are several different distinctions. There's Pearl Harbor (getting the first punch in) and then there's making sure that everybody's got fair warning. It's no fun going toe to toe with somebody if you're going to get hurt. Even if you enjoy it, even if you enjoy whatever you're talking about, fighting or guns or whatever. If I know that you're after me, that you're going to shoot me and I know that you've already said that the first time you see me you're going to shoot me, when I see you I'd shoot you first. If I tell you I'm going to shoot you before I actually pull the trigger and then walk off someplace, that's telegraphing my punches. That's something I just couldn't see anybody with any common sense doing under any set of circumstances, but it does seem to happen all the time. People say I'm going to do this or I'm going to do that and then what they're doing is some cases is they're simply working themselves into a frenzy. Or they're just lying.

Then you have to make the determination if they're lying. I mean I've had guys who say, "Well I'm going to shoot you," "I'm going to kill you," or whatever I'm going to do they're going to do, whatever they say, it wouldn't bother me a bit, because I know they're not going to. And I have other people that if they said I'm going to shoot you next time I see you, personally I would have to be sure that I saw them first because I know they're going to shoot me next time they see me. It's a difference, you have to find out who the individual is. If you don't know them then you can't afford to take the chance. It's like in a bar — if a man comes in there and gets out of hand and I'm talking to him trying to get him to straighten up, I know whether or not I'm going to have trouble with him after the first few words.

How would you tell the woofers or bluffers from the performers?

You can't take the chance. If they're an unknown quality then you can't take the chance. In other words if you don't know if the guy is going to move or not, then you go ahead and presume that he was going to move and clobber him anyway. Either that or what's going to happen is one out of every three or four times you're going to wind up getting clobbered yourself first, whether or not you overcome it is a different story, but you're going to wind up getting hurt a lot.

There is no particular mark that the woofers or bluffers have or any particular way that they act, because the action's the same. It usually starts by somebody just running his mouth and works himself into a frenzy, and then moves. Somebody, whatever they're doing, trying to get on the stage or sneak out the door with a beer. Everywhere the bar owners have trouble with that, somebody walking out the door with a beer or a mixed drink. If you have a man that's walking out a door with a beer you walk up to him and say, "Hey mister, you're not allowed to leave with a beer, I can't let you take that outside." And he says, "I bought it, I paid for it, and I'm taking it with me." Then you explain to him that it's not that you care about the beer and it's not that you care about him leaving with the beer, but the thing that you care about is that you have a lot of money invested in the business and everything is held responsible on the liquor license and if he leaves with a beer and a policeman or liquor agent sees him, you're going to get a liquor violation and it's something you could lose your license over. And that's why you don't want him to leave with the beer because you don't want to take a chance on losing your business. Now 99% of the time if you explain it to the person like that, even if they're drunk, they then understand and they'll give the beer up or stay an extra minute and drink it while they're there or they'll take a big gulp and give you the rest of it, but periodically, you'll have a guy who's a pure idot and he'll still tell you he's leaving with the beer anyway. Now if it's progressed that far and you can tell by the tone of his voice that he's going to leave with the beer, you have a choice. You can either try to wrestle him for the beer, which is stupid and silly, or you just go ahead and put him out of the picture, take the beer away from him and throw him out in the snow, because he has already determined that you're going to have trouble. The only thing is that you're the one that's deciding how it's taken care of. Now, if you let him out the door you have trouble, you're taking chance on losing your liquor license and the police department and the liquor agents, they don't care whether or why he left with it. That's not their problem. You are not allowed to let him leave. And the law's not exactly clear. I mean you have a choice and if the bar owner is 4' tall and I'm 6'8" and I'm going to leave with the beer, you know he's not going to be able to hit me in the head and take me out of the picture, but now he can pull a gun on me and say hey mister, you know, you leave the beer here. If I'm going to leave anyway then he has a choice of either shooting me or just letting me leave.

Many of these people that act like this expect that you're going to hit them. They expect to get hit, they expect a fight. They expect you to woof first. They expect a big argument and trading insults and like we did back in the school days. But the difference is that it's a business and full grown men and the school days are over and no kid problem to start with. You know they're going to get hit. I'm not interested in arguing. I've already decided what has to be done. He's not allowed to leave with a beer. That's what the law says, and it's my business, I have an investment and I have an investment to protect, and I'm jeopardizing it if I let him leave. It's the same thing with a drunk or if a guy is drunk, you say I'm sorry mister but I have to cut you off. The law says I'm not allowed to serve a drunk and you'll have to leave, you've had enough and the guy refuses to leave. The law says your liquor license is in, and what do you do if the guy refuses to leave. If you call the police department every time something happens the police department is going to close you down because you have trouble all the time.

What you have to do is either be able to talk since diplomacy is always the best, getting away from the trouble is always the best, anytime you can avoid it you let them do

97

and say whatever, the most you can accept just to get them out without the problem, but if and when it comes to the time where you know there's going to be trouble, you would be foolish not to move first.

The move to be made?

That would have a lot to do with who you thought the guy was, what you thought you could do with him. If the guy was 4' tall and weighed 90 pounds, you wouldn't have to do any more than grab him by the scuff of his shirt and his belt and just carry him out, he couldn't do anything, but if the guy's 7' tall and weights 400 pounds you really can't do that with him, so if he's going to come down what you have to do is you have to see how to hurt him as quick as you can hurt him to get him out of the picture and stop the problem without getting hurt yourself. You're not in business to get hurt.

How would you handle a normal size man?

Just knock him out. Hit him with the right hand and knock him out. If you think you're capable. Break his heart or break his spirit. Awful lot of people think they're awful tough; and they are awful tough, but you can break their spirit, you can break their heart, you can break them wanting to fight. You can take one punch every five minutes and fight for two days. But you can't take twenty in ten seconds. Just swarm all over the guy. Get it over with as fast as you can get it over with. Whatever you have to do, if it's using the billy club. the butt of a pistol, or your hand or a bottle of beer, an ashtray or the wall and the commode, just whatever's necessary to take care of the circumstances. But you have to decide yourself what's necessary. Each thing that happens is different, none of them are the same. And what you do one time is not necessarily what you would do the next time because the situation and the people are different, but the object in any case no matter what it is, whether you're in a bar yourself and somebody's bothering you or whether you're a trouble maker in a bar trying to start trouble or whether you're a bar owner or whether it's in your house or at a picnic or with your family or driving down the road, it doesn't make any difference what you're doing or who you are, it doesn't make any difference whether you're right or wrong, it's merely that if and when it comes time for you to have some kind of trouble, physical trouble that's going to involve some kind of fighting, whether knives, guns, fists, an ashtray or a bottle of beer, once you make the determination that it's necessary that something is going to happen, then you decide whatever you think that you have to do to win in order to sustain the least amount of injury to yourself. I would rather have a skinned knuckle than a skinned nose. And most of the time if you get a skinned nose you also get a skinned knuckle. Because you're trading off.

Because if he hits me I'm going to hit him back. But if I have a choice I'm only going to have a skinned knuckle. I'm not going to have a skinned nose and the way to do that is when you decide that something has to be done and something is going to happen, then you just do it. Whatever it is is you just do it.

Would you say that most of the time when this sort of thing happens, like when somebody starts woofing and you just do it, the other guy is really not prepared for it, in other words, he's expecting you to woof some more?

Most of the time, he doesn't understand what he's doing. I'd have to say that's probably the biggest thing. People actually don't understand what they're doing when they do it.

Back to the example of the bar, but you can apply it any way you want to apply it. They don't understand that they are jeopardizing your liquor license. They don't understand that they're jeopardizing your livelihood. They don't understand that they're running off your business and the most important is they don't understand or don't care. It really is immaterial which one of the two it is, whether they don't understand or whether they don't care because the end result is the same. They are jeopardizing your liquor license, they are jeopardizing your livelihood, they are running your customers off. People come in to have a good time, party, and have fun. They don't want to see a fight. They don't want some guy just screaming and hollering and making an ass out of himself or doing handstands in the middle of the floor. That's not what the bars are for and that's not what they came to see or do.

The end result is the same so you just have to take them out if they fall into either one of those categories. You might as well go ahead and start swinging. If and only if you're not intelligent enough or don't have the facilities to get rid of the problem without it becoming something physical.

Often the other fellow doesn't have the intelligence to comprehend the situation. I find it periodically myself and I know other people that find it all the time, but I also know that in any given situation somebody can handle it without there being a problem. In other words, there has to be something that you can say or something that you can do in order to make the guy understand or behave.

Could you elaborate on the diplomatic approach?

What a peace maker is or your diplomacy part is, is in trying to figure out what will cool the situation without violence and in almost any given situation you should be able to do that in some way. It does not mean that you have the mental or physical ability to do it verbally, and those are the cases that you have to handle physically since you're either not intelligent enough to figure out what to say and how to say it, or what to do or how to do it.

One night I had a guy in the bar, a black guy who was drunk. He works at a service station, he wears a service station's uniform and he's not a bad guy and he got more than he should drink. One minute he's walking around and as long as he was walking around he was fine, but after he sat down for a few minutes he went to sleep. I woke him up and he couldn't quite get himself together and he didn't want to be bothered, he just wanted to sit there and sleep. I tried a number of different things in talking to him like, "Hey mister, you're not allowed to sleep in here," and "You have to pull yourself up," or "You have to sit up straight, you have to or why don't you walk around a little bit," or "Why don't you go home," or "You've had enough and I have to ask you to leave," and he just sits there and mumbles.

If you find yourself in the position I was in you have to consider alternatives. What you've tried so far doesn't work and you have to go another step further someway. It's either bodily picking him up, helping him to the door and if you do that he may resent the fact that you put your hands on him and may decide to fight over that. The fact that you put your hands on him, in which case then you have a physical problem already, and the last thing that you ever want to do is to cause a physical problem yourself which you might be doing if you put your hands on him, although that would be in the case something that you would try before you would physically try to throw him out.

My conversation with this guy did not work, nothing that I had to say got a response from him until I explained to him that it was a violation of the liquor laws. It's not that I cared, but I was afraid of losing my liquor license and that if the police walked in and saw him they would immediately take him to jail for being drunk, which that would be his problem and I'm not worried about you going to jail, that's your fault because I've already told you, but the police department would give me a citation for allowing a drunk in my bar or somebody that's intoxicated in which case that would go against my liquor license and subject to cost me my liquor license. When I explained that to him it kind of dawned on him what he was doing. As far as he's concerned he's just sitting at the bar sleeping and it is no big deal to him. He works in a service station or he works in a factory or whatever he does, it's no big deal to him, he gets drunk a lot of times and goes to sleep and that's all he's doing. You have to make him understand that he is doing more than what he thinks he is doing. He is jeopardizing your livelihood, jeopardizing your bar and your station in life, not by what he's doing but the consequences of what he's doing. The things that he doesn't see. By explaining that to him they guy picked himself up and pulled himself together and walked out the door. Now I don't know what happened to him, he just left, I didn't have any trouble with him.

How often do you run into a case where somebody just comes in and just wants to be a hard nose?

Not very often. One in the last seven month period, just once. The individual thought he was big enough and strong enough to do whatever he wanted to do in the bar and he was willing to whip anybody that was willing to stop him. That guy I put out in the street with his hands broken. That was just an out and out confrontation. I don't find if very often because I'm so well known and I'm so big. For a normal guy to walk into a bar and go against somebody that's put together half way decently, 6'8" and weight 260 pounds, doesn't make much sense. I personally don't get challenged that often, but I know other bar owners that do, and most of the time what happens is the guy does whatever he wants to do because the bar owner figures the only choice that he has is to either call the police, which gets him in trouble, or get a baseball bat, or get two or three of his friends and together whip the guy to get him out, or shoot him, or pull a gun on him. And the lesser of all the evils sometimes is just to let the guy do whatever he wants to do.

Could you give us some more examples of diplomacy as opposed to violence?

You have to use a lot of diplomacy anytime you deal with the public. If you were in line getting theater tickets, let's say you and your wife were going out to dinner and you decided to go to the show first and you were standing in line and some guy comes from all the way in the back of the line and walked right past everybody and jumped right in front of the line in front of you. That's not right at all, and you have to decide whether or not you should do something about it. Or let's say you were in the grocery store and you were going through the check-out line and you have some man or some woman come up with a whole armload of packages and just jump right in front of you, what do you do about it? What do you normally do? What would I normally do? Nothing.

The difference is that I am a customer, it would bother me, I would not like it and if it happened consistently I would no longer patronize that grocery store, that restaurant, that movie theater or whatever. I would go somewhere else because I don't have to take that kind of treatment.

Suppose everytime you went to the grocery store you were going to have people jumping in line in front of you and instead of waiting five minutes in line you're going to wait twenty minutes in line everytime because people just are going to jump in front of you, it's going to happen fairly regular. The reason I put it that way is so that you understand what the customer's feelings are. Or, if you and your wife went out to dinner in a restaurant and some guy just starts hollering and screaming and cussing out loud, one time you might overlook it, but it would still bother you if he's standing in front of your wife, I know you would feel that you should say something or you should do something; but if you do you know you're subject to get in trouble, get into a fight, get hurt, not be able to support your kids or go to jail. You as a customer have to make that determination, but the man that is really caught in the middle is the owner of that business because it's his job to see that that doesn't happen, it's his job not to allow that person to get by with whatever he's doing. Now if he's jumping in line what he has got to do is he's got to walk up to that person and in some kind of way he has got to get that person to go back to the end of the line. And to the best of his ability he should and would use all the diplomacy that he could and you personally would sigh with relief when you see the owner of a supermarket come up to the woman who just jumped in front of the line and say, "Lady, this man was in line first, you go to the back of the line." Now if she refuses to go he has to make another determination. What does he do then? Some kind of way says he's already made that stand and he should stop it unless the woman would give him a very legitimate reason, in which case he would ask you, "Would it be alright if this woman, you know, her baby's sick and she has to go to the doctor," or "She's just got a prescription or whatever it is, and normally you would say, "Well yes, go ahead." Then it doesn't bother you. Then it no longer bothers you. But if, let's say you're going to a movie, you and your wife, and you have a couple young

103

guys, 18, 19 years old, you're going to see a new movie that's out, "Jaws," you're going to see "Jaws" and you've got a couple young guys who just run up and jump right in front of you and then here comes the owner and the owner says, "Hey you two guys have to get back in the back of the line." Now what does he do if those two guys refuse to get out of that line? He has a multitude of choices. He can stop them from buying the tickets. He can tell the ticket girl, you don't sell these guys tickets, he can let them continue on, he can ask you since you're behind them if it's alright if they got up there.

He may say, "You know mister, I know what these two guys have done is wrong, it's not right any way, but I think if I try to put them back in the back of the line I'm going to have serious trouble trying to do it, I'm going to have a fight or something and I really don't need a fight and all that trouble. Would it be alright with you if I just, you know, let's let them go on and maybe we won't have any trouble out of them." So then you have to say, "Well, I don't really want to have a fight either, I'm out to have a nice time with my wife, I'm going to the movie," so you'd probably say, "What the hell, let them go ahead."

If a friend of yours comes up and jumps right in, it's the same thing, he's jumping line. It may be fine with me and you but it's not fine with everybody else that's behind us. It makes a difference though because if say you and I are here and here comes a friend and gets in front of us, it's not like a direct insult to the guy that's behind us. He may not like it, but it's not an insult. A fellow named Hatfield in prison stabbed a guy down in Atlanta over that. Some jig got in front of him and Hatfield says, "Hey, you're not supposed to cut in front of me," and this jig said, "*&†+," this that and the other. Hatfield went and got a knife and came back and just as they were passing the hamburgers Hatfield got him and dumped him right onto the grill, blood all over the place and everybody screaming, "Don't get the blood on the hamburgers!" but that wasn't the same situation if Hatfield had say you and me in front of him and somebody had cut in front of you like a friend of ours, I don't think it would have bothered him, I don't think it ever bothered me, as long as they didn't do it ten or fifteen at a time. It's when the guy cuts in front of you personally.

One of the things that happened in Terre Haute, especially like on the phone lines, and that's when they were out in the halls, or any type of line there, is actually I never had anybody cut in front of me. They would pick the weak sister. Here's some guy that looks weak, they would cut in front of him and then it's on him, it's not my fight because if there's a guy in front of me and he's weak and the guy that bucks on him is weak, it's not my place to step in front of him and say, "Hey don't be cutting in front of this guy, you know," that's his problem.

If you have to get physical should you say anything first?

Let's say the owner of the supermarket, the owner of the restaurant, or the owner or manager in any case of the movie theater, has to make a determination. He goes up and talks to these guys and they say, "Hey man, fuck off, we're not going back to the back of the line, we're going in," now what does he do? He has tried all verbal methods that he is mentally capable of throwing at these guys trying to talk them into getting out of line and going back to the end of the line. He's done all that he could do, then he has to make the determination of whether or not he's going to back down from it or whether he's going to do something about it. Now, if he is going to do something physical, his move is not to say, "Okey then we're going to have to fight," or "Now you're going to move or else I'm going to move you." He should have already made the determination and he should have already eliminated all those before he decided that it was necessary to do something physical. And if it is necessary to do something physical then what he should have done is just knocked their brains out and carried them to the back of the line. They would not do it again and he would have not got hurt and everybody in the place would have said, "Well it had to be done." Those guys are complete idiots and they never gave him any choice, they jumped in the front of the line, they refused to get out, he talked to them real nice. He did everything, he actually begged them, asked them please get out of the line, and when he did everything that he could do, he just knocked them both out.

Would you consider that a Pearl Harboring?

I wouldn't consider it that and I don't thing you would, but I think most people standing in line would because they wouldn't be expecting it, they would expect people to be woofing and getting themselves geared up. Now that wasn't a pearl harbor to you and it shouldn't have been to them, but it might be to others because they were not expecting it.

If you have been in a movie line, going to the movie and it would have happened to two or three guys in front of you, you would have overhead everything that was said. You would know there was an argument or a discussion and the owner of the place had to come out and try to get these guys from bucking line and all that kind of stuff and they refuse and he's tried to talk them out of it and they refuse to leave and refuse to do what they're supposed to do, and he finally winds up and knocks their brains out, you know, what do you do then. You don't do anything. Just stand clear. Everybody would say the same thing, they had it coming to them, they had it coming, but those guys knew they were asking for trouble when they did it in the first place. I mean, they started it. They put you in the position where you had to do something about it and then you gave them a chance of remedying the whole situation without any problem, all they had to do was walk out of the line and go back to the back of the line. What I am saying is that basically the way to handle this thing with diplomacy is to allow them to save face. You can't just go out there and say, "Hey you two punks, get in the back of the line," then you've practically committed yourself to a fight. Then if they are strong individuals in their own right you're going to have trouble and your trouble is going to be serious. If they're weak, then they'll go to the back of the line. Any line in the world some people would walk to the front of the line. Even a weak sister. And if you called him down on it he'd probably say, "*&%%$+††," he'd get loud and boisterous. Now if you

106

don't know him you have to make the determination, man I'm going to have trouble with this guy. Say for example, he's a weight lifter and all that, he weighs over 200 pounds, you know, what the hell am I going to do with him. So now, what I would do with this guy is I would just knock his brains out and then drag him off, throw him out the door, drag him off to the side or whatever and let the line go on after I tried to talk to him and by talking to him I would find out that he's an idiot and as soon as I came to that determination and I know by talking to him that I'm not going to get him to do what I have to get him to do and that he's either going to completely disrupt my business, my whole entire business , or we're going to have a hell of a fight, I don't want to have a fight, if I have to whip him I want to be able to win and whip him without getting hurt myself as quickly as possible because I have a business to run.

It's the same thing whether or not it's on a personal basis or whether you're a customer in a bar, if I walked into a bar and I sat down and somebody was bothering me, I would get up and move and if they came back over there I'll try to talk to them but as soon as, whether it's before I talk to them or when they first come up to me, then whatever it is, according to what they do, as soon as I determine in my own mind that I am going to have trouble with them because I cannot get out of it, or I am going to have trouble with him because he has done something serious enough to me for me to say that I have to have trouble with him. If he walked up and mistreated my girlfriend or my wife or something or one of my kids, then I would have to make a determination right there and then, "Hey this guy has already went further than I would allow him," so I'm going to have to have trouble with him. Or if I tried to avoid any trouble and he continued on, wherever I am at the time when I have to do something then I'm going to move as strong and as hard as I feel the situation calls for.

Now what you do in a situation where you have to move like that but you're not just facing one individual, you're facing maybe anywhere from three to ten, how do you move then?

The first thing you look for is the position of strength. See who the strongest one is. Not necessarily because usually the strongest one, there are exceptions to it, but usually the strongest people there are not the ones that cause all the trouble, it's almost always the idiot that causes the trouble and just because they're an idiot doesn't make them tough. The idiots are always the ones that start the trouble. And they're the weak ones. If let's say that you and some friends went out with an idiot and the idiot got all the way out of hand and you know he's an idiot and you know he's doing wrong and you didn't know me and I just drilled him, just knocked his brains out and now he's laying on the floor bleeding and there are you and your friends. I'm standing with my back against the wall and I've got a baseball bat in my hands, you know, I just knocked the idiot's head in and I say, "Now fellas, you saw it and I don't want any trouble with you, take your friend and leave," now what are you going to do, charge the baseball bat?

What if your friends and one idiot walk in the bar and the idiot got out of hand? Normally what I would do is try to come talk to you and the idiot or you and another friend and say, "Hey, your friend is getting out of hand, please take care of him, stop him from doing what he's doing, I can't allow it," so now you're on the spot.

Your reaction, if logical, would be like this: I could either say you're out of line and if the man hits you, and I could say it loud enough for everybody to hear, if the man hurts you, you had it coming don't bother us, alright, or I would say, "Okey, you're coming with us, you're out of line," and that would be the end of it. There's no way it could ever come back on you with a situation like that with diplomacy because you've allowed us to save face but here this guy's getting out of line and maybe I don't know anything about it and my friends don't know anything about it and the next thing I know he's laying on the floor and you're standing over him with a pistol and even if I find out later that he had it coming it was on you to come to me first.

That's where we're talking about using the diplomacy. And anytime you can use, any time you can avoid doing it yourself you're better off. If the guy is with somebody, if he knows somebody in the place, you're much better off going to them first and seeing whether or not they can handle it. You could get wild and drunk and all that kind of stuff and your friend could probably still have a chance of talking to you and talking some sense into you. If you were already mad hot and you were drunk or whatever, the heat might make you do something because you really don't care about me, we're not friends. Your friend could at least get close enough to you and talk to you.

Or if a friend came to me in something like that, even if I was so mad that I wanted to kill you right there, if a friend came to me and said, "Look, this isn't right, as a favor to me would you just cool it and let it go," I'd have to because he's with me and I don't have any choice. Even if I walk out of there and I want to get a bazooka to come back and finish you off, since it's from my friend that has to be the end of it.

How do most fights start and what is the best way to handle them? What do most people do wrong?

What people do is they don't make the determination that they're going to have trouble, what they do is they argue and fuss and evolve into a fight and then they're both prepared and they're both geared up and they're both going to have many bruises and those for many days. It's only necessary for one person to have them as long as you have a choice, you'd rather the other man got them.

When two countries are at war they've already determined that they're going to have trouble with each other. When the Japanese attacked Pearl Harbor we knew that we had trouble with the Japanese. We had already determined that we're going to have trouble with the Japanese because they had attacked Pearl Harbor, you don't tell them, "Hey tomorrow at 10:00 we're hitting Iwojima or Nagasaki," or "Tomorrow at 6:00 in the evening or come daylight we're going to have the battle of the Coral Sea," you don't tell them anything. The object is to catch them with their pants down and do the greatest amount of damage that you can to them with the least amount of trouble or whatever to yourself, and the only difference between a war between two countries and a fight between two individuals is what the determination is. Once a country has decided that they are going to have a war with another country they don't tell that other country anything, they sneak and they probe and they don't tell anybody they are going to hit the beach at Normandy. Even on an individual basis once the determination is made that you are going to have trouble with the other man you're going to go to war, you don't tell him anything.

Could you sum up your whole philosophy of hand-to-hand combat in one paragraph?

Let's say you're in position, you know already you're going to have trouble with someone, you've decided that in your own mind for whatever reason, right, wrong, indifferent, it doesn't make any difference, you know that you're going to have physical trouble with someone, what do you do? What is your move? Are you going to be verbal, are you going to say, "Hey you, I'm going to whip you"? No. You only have one shot and that's hitting him as hard as you can as fast as you can and hoping he can't recover in time to hurt you. That's the whole philosophy.